Psalms
Through my eyes

<u>Introduction</u>

I want to start by saying that this book is not a reading of Psalms. Instead, it is Psalms, through my eyes. What this means, is that these were the words that came to me as I was reading these specific Psalms. My hope is that this book helps you grow, and lets you know that no matter what season of life you are in, Christ can always be found. I hope that this book helps you see how good God is, that He loves you, and that He is with you through your pain and suffering. God shelters you, protects you, and He loves you, with a perfect love. This book is a book of Psalms

Through my eyes

This book was based off of Psalms 23, 37, 40, 42, 46, 56, 61, & 91

Please note: Because these were written through my eyes, please remember that this was written in current time, which is now after the death and resurrection of Jesus Christ.

Table of contents

Psalm 42
Through my eyes

My soul hungers and thirsts for you, my God, and my friend. When I awake, I need you, and when I sleep, I need you still. You sustain me Lord. If I go a day without reading, I miss your words. I need you more than food, more than life itself. Only You God, sustain me, and only You God, give me life. I am however, sorrowful. Tears run down my face often, and I wonder, how much longer God? I try so hard to walk in your ways, I try so hard to please you, yet my tears speak of sorrow and pain.

When I remember my pain and my sorrows, I pour out my soul within me. I used to follow my own paths, and I never asked what Your will was, but now, I know of the only way that I will ever need to go. Now I know, that it's your path that I seek. I will follow no other. When I get weary, I may say, let me go this way or that, but then you soothe my aching heart, and You remind me that You are good. You remind me that although narrow, there is no path like Yours God, as there is no god like You God. No one can right my wrongs like You, protect me like You, comfort me like You, calm my fears like You, give me strength like You, redeem me like You, die for me, like You.

I know that my life is in You, my life is through You. I know that You love me Lord, and I know Your plans for me are good. So why my soul, are you so worried within me? Why are you so filled with sorrow? Put your hope in God, for I shall yet praise Him. For the Lord, He is my hope and my salvation. His face shines upon me, and gives me hope. My God will help me.

Why my soul, are you so worried within me? Do you not remember, our faithful God? Do you not remember the time when He saved your family from a possibly fatal car crash on the highway? Do you not remember when God saved your family from that drunk driver on the road? Do you not remember God giving you peace that surpasses all understanding? Do you not remember when God saved you from your anxious thoughts? Do you not remember when God made a way, when there seemed to be no way? Do you not remember when God gave you strength? Do you remember? Do you remember when God saved you? When He died for you?

Therefore, when my soul is saddened, and worried within me, I will recall of Your faithfulness, my God and my Friend.

The winds and waves have gone over me. You are my God, and they obey Your every command. Therefore, I will not be swept away by the waves of this life, for you are their Maker, and You are my Friend. Your lovingkindness is with me when I am awake, and I sing your songs as I sleep, for you are with me when I rise and when I slumber. You have never left my side, not for but a moment. You are the God of my life, and there is none like You.

There is no rock, like my Rock, and there is no god, like my God. One who loves His children the way He does, and calms the storms as He. For who can you say, breaks you on the Rock, only to build you up stronger again? Who thinks of you, more than the grains of sand, and Who knew you, before you came to be? Who made you have a purpose, and brought you from your despair? Was it not the Lord your God?

So why my soul, why so worried and depressed within me? Your anxious thoughts, leave less room for your hope. Hope in God, for I shall yet praise Him. His deliverance is inevitable. You will see, and you shall praise Him for all of His goodness, mercy, and love. You Lord, are the only hope of my sorrow, my God.

Psalm 46
Through my eyes

I seek You God. I seek you when I am afraid, and I seek you when I feel lost. When I feel lost, I know that I am never lost to You. You are my place of refuge, my strong tower, and my strength. You shelter me, and You guard me. When I am in trouble, Your arms secure me. Therefore, I will not fear, I will not be afraid, depressed, nor anxious. Even if this whole world, were to be removed from its place, my hope is still in You. You will still guide me, save me, and protect me in Your loving arms. If the mountains, were thrown into the midst of the sea, You will still be my Protector, and my Friend. And even though the waters around me rage, and the seas sweep over me, yet they will not consume me, for You are my God. The mountains may shake, and my life may be as if it were in ruins, but You God, are my Maker. You know how to put me back together again, therefore, I will trust in You. Though the pieces of me are scattered, only You Lord, know where to find them.

Even though the storms around me are many, and the weight of this life so heavy, there is a place where I can always find the calm of these storms. That place Lord, is in You. When my soul is weary, I look to my Father. In Jesus, I find my peace. Waters may be raging around me, yet there is always a calm river that flows through them, one that I can only find in You. You Jesus, are in the midst of me. You go before me, behind me, and all around me. You Lord, are my secret hiding place. I hide in the shelter of Your wings, and there I find peace. Your Spirit gives me strength, and guides me with love and peace. God, You are my Anchor. Therefore, I can not be moved, because you Lord, can not be moved. You say, "*Therefore I tell you, whatever you ask for in prayer, believe that you have received it, and it will be yours.*" Lord, you tell us to believe, and to have faith, and that without faith, it is impossible to please You. Therefore, I will believe, and my heart will remain steadfast. I will not let the winds move me, because my Anchor will be secure, as I know where my hope comes from. In You Lord, I dwell in safety. I declare to You, my Lord and my God, that You will help me. You will not leave me alone, and You will work all things for my good. This I believe with my whole heart.

The whole earth could rage and be against me. Everything around me may seem against me Lord, but You, can calm them with a word. No word returns to You empty, and You alone Lord, can calm this storm in me.

You are the God of Jacob, Issac, and Abraham. You Lord, are my Friend and my refuge. You Lord, are with me.

Let us all see the works of the Lord. He brings up, and He tares down. He alone makes wars cease. Was it not God, who made the Egyptians wheel fall off? Was it not God, who sheltered by day and night? Was it not God, who delivered His people? Who is it then, that can deliver

from the hand of the Lord? Who could thwart His plans?
There is not one. Therefore, be still, and know, that He is
God.
He will be exalted among the nations, and before Him,
every knee shall bow.

Psalm 56
Through my eyes

God, please show me mercy. There are those around me, who treat me harshly. I try hard Lord, to push past them, but they try to push me down. Lord, please show me mercy. I know I am not perfect, but I try hard to please You. I know that wrath does not please You, and I try to show others mercy and grace, but there are many who come against me. Help me walk in a manner worthy of You Lord. In a manner that pleases You.

Father, there are times when I am afraid. I know that I am but dust, and You are God, my God. You made this earth, and You formed my frame. There is none who can take Your place, because there has, is, and will never be anyone like You. For who can suspend the clouds in the sky, and not let them fall under the weight of the waters? Therefore, I will not burst under their weight either, for I put my trust in You. Even in the darkest moments, I will praise You. Even when my voice is gone, I will still praise You. I will remember Your words, and You will be my help, my Sustainer. God, You are my God, and I put my trust in You. When I feel afraid, I will choose faith, instead of fear. There is no one who holds His children, like You God. You hold us in the palm of your hands. Jesus, You told us this, *"I give them eternal life, and they shall never perish; no one will snatch them out of my hand. My Father, who has given them to me, is greater than all; no one can snatch*

them out of my Father's hand. I and the Father are one."
No one can take me from You Lord. Therefore, I know
that I am safe with You. I am safe in Your hands, always.
People twist my words, they talk behind my back, and
their thoughts toward me are evil. They say things that
they ought not, and they seek to oppress me. They try to
tare me down with their words, and they wait as a
serpent, waiting to strike. My Lord, and my Redeemer,
You will protect me. You are judge, and I am not.
Therefore, I will keep my eyes on You. I will not be
distracted by those who seek my ruin. My hope will
remain in You Lord.

Sometimes Lord, I feel as if I am wandering aimlessly.
Lord, only You, can number those wanderings. My tears
also are many, and if I were to fill them, they would
become a large body of water. My tears are many, but
only You Lord, can place them in Your bottle. They are in
Your book Lord. Although my tears are many, and my
sorrows plenty, I know that You will deliver me out of
them all. I know Lord, that You always make my enemies
turn back, because You are for me. I will continually
praise You, and praise Your words, and even in sorrow, I
have put my trust in You. I will not be afraid, for what can
man do to me? You are with me always, and none can
surpass You Lord. Therefore, what do I have to fear?

My words to You are true. I will praise you Lord, for You
have delivered me. You have widened my path, and kept
my feet from falling. If it was not for You Lord, my feet

would have slipped. You have strengthened me in despair, and have lifted me up in my time of need. Thank You God, for You are always faithful and true. Therefore my mouth, will never cease praising You.

Psalm 61
Through my eyes

God, I am in despair. Hear my cry Lord. Let my weeping reach Your ears, for to the end of the earth, I will cry to You. My heart Lord, is overwhelmed. It is weighted, as if a large rock has fallen upon it. Lord, lead me to the Rock that is higher than I. A Rock more powerful than the one weighted on my chest. For who could ever compare to You Lord? You have been my shelter. You have covered me in my times of need, and You alone, have been my refuge, my safe place of hiding. Darkness can not find me here in Your arms. You are my strong tower, and You hide me from the enemy. I will remain in You, as You remain in me. I will come to You as I cry out, and I will remain in Your tabernacle from now until all eternity. I will trust in Your shelter. Your wings they hide me. Your wings they comfort me. I am safe with You.

You God, have heard my vows, and You have given me an inheritance that none other can give. You have marked out my days, and for all those days I will follow You, my Lord and my God. I will abide in You forever.

My God, give us all mercy and truth, which may preserve us!

I will sing praises to You Lord, and I will lift Your name up forever. I will keep my promises to You Lord, and always praise Your name.

I will sing praises... You will lift Your name up
forever I will lift... oh you are my Lord, and always
praise Your name

Psalm 91
Through my eyes

I dwell in the secret place of the Most High. He is my
Father, and I am His daughter. I remain under the shadow
of my Father, the Almighty. My Father is my Lord, He is
my refuge and my fortress, my strong tower and my
protector. He is faithful. He has never failed me before,
and I know that He never will. He is my God, and I can,
and I will trust Him. At all times, through all seasons. Even
in difficult ones, I will ask Him for His mercy and grace,
and to give me eyes to see, and to help me remember
that He is good. To remember that He works all things to
its proper end, and He works all things together for my
good, even the unpleasant things. He will perfect that
which concerns me.

I know that He will deliver me from the trap of the
enemy, and from the deadly plague. My Father is the best
Father that I could ever ask for. He loves me so much,
that He covers me with His beautiful, radiant feathers.
There truly is none like Him. None that can protect me
and love me the way that He does. As a baby chick runs
under the mother hen's wings, so shall I, run to Him, for
my Father is my refuge. He shelters me in storms, and
hides me under the safety of His wings. In Him I find
peace. There is none like my Father. He is the strongest
there is, was, or ever will be. If ever I am afraid, or have
any other emotions that do not fit who I am in Christ, I

will remember His truth. The words on a page, that are more than just words on a page, but words that I hold close and dear to my heart. They are my shield and buckler. They protect me from the enemies lies, and from his fiery arrows. One without Christ has no power to withstand the enemy, but Christ lives in me, so whom shall I fear? For who could go against my God? There is not one. And my God lives within me, so I will not be afraid. God has given me all authority over the enemy, so I will not fear.

I will not be afraid of bad dreams, sleepless nights, and overthinking as I lay my head, nor will I be afraid of any other terrors of the night, nor by day. I will not be afraid of the enemies arrows, nor of the plague that walks in darkness. A plague destroys, but my Father gives. And He gave me this armor to protect me, because He loves me. Therefore, the destruction that seems to be coming, I will not be afraid of, because my Father is with me. Whether I am brought high or low, He is still there. He never leaves my side, for He is good, and He is God. Why should anyone fear, when God, is for them? Perhaps one may fear if a mere human were by their side in battle, but with God by your side in battle, what is there to be afraid of? Instead, I will be still, and know, that He is God.

If a thousand people die at my side, and ten thousand people die at my right hand, it will still not come near me. Destruction may be near my feet, but my Father has shielded me, because He loves me, and because I am His.

I will only look with my eyes, at the fallen beside me, and see the reward of the wicked.

I have made my Father, the LORD, who is my place of hiding, my refuge. He is even the Most High, and none compare, and none go above or before Him. Because I have made Him the place in which I dwell, no evil shall happen to me, nor shall any plague come near me, nor my family, because we belong to the LORD. My God is above all things. He rules over all and is in charge of all things. Therefore, He has put His angels in charge of me, to protect me and keep me safe, to keep me in all my ways, and protect me in all I do. In the angels hands, they will lift me up, so I don't dash my foot against a stone. I am lifted high above the enemy, therefore, I will walk on the enemy, with him underfoot. I will not only walk, but I will trample. I will trample all of my enemies under my feet, because my God has given me all authority to do so. As an ant is trampled under foot, so will be my enemies.

I love my Father, with true love. One that is not conditional and based on circumstances. I love Him for better or worse. And because I have set this love upon Him, He will deliver me. He will set me on high, because I know His name, and because I believe in His Son, who graciously gave His own life, to save mine. When I call on my Father He will answer me, because He loves me with such a perfect love. He will be with me when I am in trouble, no matter how small, nor how great, He is with me in all trouble. My Father is my protector. He delivers me and honors me. I belong to Him. Bought with a price, I am His, and He is mine. With long life, He will satisfy me. He has shown me His salvation, through His Son, Jesus Christ, who gave His life for mine.

Psalm 23
Through my eyes

Lord, You alone are my Shepherd. With You as my Shepherd, I shall want for nothing. All that I need, may be found in You. Goodness and mercy shall follow me all the days of my life, and I will dwell in Your house forever. Even when my soul is overwhelmed, and life's waves have raged around me, You Lord, always lead me beside still waters. You sustain me Lord. You Lord, always keep me in perfect peace. You Lord, make me safe. You restore my weary soul, and lead me in the paths of righteousness, for Your name's sake. The paths that You have chosen for Your children, are always good. You would never lead me down a path that was not for my good. Therefore, I trust You. Lead me Lord, down the path that is for my good, and for Your glory.

Even though I walk through valleys too dark to see, I will not fear, for You are with me. The valley may seem scary, but it's just a shadow. They may try to scare me, but they have no authority over Your children, for we belong to You Lord. Whatever shadows may try to scare us, they can always be broken up with Your light Lord. My eyes are to always remain on You, for only You can light the darkness which surrounds me. When I fight Lord, I will fight on my knees, hands lifted high. For You are worthy of my praise. You fight for me Lord, and You would never abandon me. Therefore, I will not be afraid of the turmoil which surrounds me. Perhaps if I were walking alone, then I would fear, but Lord, You are always with me, so why should I fear? There is no where that I could go, that You won't find me. You are with me always. Whether the depths of the sea, or the darkest valley, Your rod and Your staff, Lord, they comfort me. You are my good Shepherd. You guide me and lead me. Your staff is a symbolism of your authority over Your sheep. You Lord, we belong to You. You bought us with a price, and no one can take us from Your hands. Therefore, the shadows will not overtake me, and I will not be afraid. I choose, not to be afraid.

Even though there are many who seek my destruction, I will not worry about them. Instead, I will eat in safety, at the table in which You have prepared for me. I am safe with You Lord. Enemies could be all around me, shouting my destruction, yet, I will keep my eyes on You, for You Lord, keep me in perfect peace. You bless me and satisfy me with all that I will ever need. My Lord and my God. Only in You Lord, do I dwell in safety. I know that goodness and mercy will follow me, all the days of my life. I know this Lord, because it is You that gives good things. All good gifts come from You Lord. I am Yours. I am Your child, and You are the perfect Father, so I stand on Your promises, and I know Lord, that Your goodness and mercy will follow me, all the days of my life. I will dwell with You always Lord. In Your house, I will dwell, in safety.

Psalm 37
Through my eyes

I will not be worried because of those who do evil. I will also not be jealous when those who do wrong, succeed in their ways. Although they may seem to be prosperous for a little while, they will soon be cut off, and cast into the fire.

Instead, I will trust in You Lord. I will trust in You, even when I can not see. Even when the waters rage around me, and I feel as if I can not breathe, still, I will trust in You. You Lord, hold my head above water. You will not let me drown. I will overcome evil, and I will do good. Therefore, even if I feel as if I am drowning, I will use what seems to be my last breath, to do good. To honor You Lord. To please You Lord. I will dwell in Your house all the days of my life, and I will trust in Your faithfulness. As surely as I drink and eat to stay alive, I too, will lean on Your faithfulness to sustain me. I will remain steadfast, and I will trust in the God that I know You are. I know You are good, You are trustworthy and true. I take great pleasure in You Lord, my Rock and my firm foundation. Lord, You know the things I wish for, and You know the things I need. Only You Lord, can lead me down the right paths. I will trust in You to give me the desires of my heart.

My way, is Yours O God. My path I have laid down, to follow one better. There is no path better than Yours God. Your paths and ways are higher than mine. Therefore, my way is Yours, to do with as You please. I will trust in You, and I will trust that You will finish what You have started in me. You will not abandon me, and You are faithful to complete it. At times I become sorrowful Lord, waiting day and night for You to deliver us. I say, how long Lord? But then, You strengthen me, and remind me that those who wait patiently on You, will not be put to shame. Those who wait on You Lord, You will renew their strength, They shall mount up with wings like eagles, They shall run and not be weary, They shall walk and not faint. Therefore, I will rest in You Lord. I will wait patiently for You, even when my soul is overwhelmed, and sorrow has reached my eyes, even still, I will wait. You will deliver us, because You are just. Only I ask, please Lord, when my soul is overwhelmed, lead me to the Rock that is higher than I. Only in You Lord, do I find my peace.

I will not worry when others wicked schemes come to pass, and when they prosper in their ways. I will not be angry, as I know Lord, anger does not please You. Therefore, I will put away all wrath, as it only causes harm. For what does my anger do to the wicked? Does it not only harm myself? Does it not only displease You Lord? Therefore, I will move away from wrath, and instead, put my trust in You, the One who makes all things right.

Those who do evil shall be cut off. But not those who wait on You Lord. Those who wait on You, will inherit the earth. You have graciously given Your children an inheritance. Through You Jesus, we have eternal life. Through You, we are blessed to be called children of the Most High. Although Lord, if You were not in this eternal life, then I would not want to be there. For I do not seek the streets of gold, although beautiful, because Lord, You are my desire.

You Lord, give me peace. When my soul is overwhelmed, and I cry out to You God, shower me with peace that passes all understanding. Where would I be Lord, without Your peace? Where would I be Lord, without You?

The wicked plot against the just Lord. The wicked seek to destroy, but Lord, You laugh at them. For who is he who believes that he can stand up to You, and to Your people? He is naive to think that he could stand against the Lord Almighty. You Lord, see his future, because You Lord, know all. You see the end of the wicked, and You know that there day is coming, therefore, You laugh at Him. The wicked draw their sword, they bend their bow, and look to destroy the poor and needy. To cast down those who are in need. They seek to devour those who do what's right Lord. But, I will not worry, because I know that their sword shall enter their own heart, and with Your mighty outstretched arm, their bows will be broken.

I would rather have little and have You Lord. I would rather have little and have You, than to have everything, and not know You. Because to me Lord, You are everything. Therefore in my eyes, having less, is but gain to me. For what will these earthly riches do for me in the end? Will they come with me to receive my inheritance? These earthly riches will be worthless, and futile. It is better to know You Jesus, for You are my eternal security, and no riches could ever compare to You Lord. Money and riches of this world, could never buy the kind of love that You have given me. Your love Lord, is precious to me. It can never be bought nor earned, as You freely give it. Jesus, through Your death and resurrection, You have made me free. Even our faith Lord, is a gift from You. Because You are a good God, and because You love us. Despite our faults and sins, You love us, and You died for us. What riches are worth more than this kind of love? I say not one.

The arms of the wicked shall be broken, but You Lord, uphold the righteous. With Your mighty right hand, You withhold them. Therefore, I will not fear, nor be dismayed, for You are my God. You will strengthen me, and You Lord, will help me. You will uphold me with Your righteous right hand, because You God, are good.

Lord, You know the days of the upright, and our inheritance shall be forever, for all eternity. Even through times of evil, we will not be ashamed, and even though famine may come, we shall still be satisfied. You Lord, always provide and sustain. In You alone Lord, we are satisfied.

But not so the wicked. The wicked shall perish, and the enemies of the Lord, shall vanish. Into the pit of fire, they shall vanish.

The wicked only takes. They borrow, and they do not repay. But the righteous show mercy, and they give, even when they don't have much to give. When we see someone in need, we are to show mercy and give. Is not everything you own the Lord's anyway? Show God gratitude for all that you have, by giving to those in need. For what little we own, we share, and what little we have to eat, that too, we share. To bless others is to bless us, and to bless others, is to glorify God.

My steps are ordered by the Lord, and He delights in my way. I may plan my steps, but it is the Lord who establishes them. At this, I rejoice. For who knows the way of the created, better than the Creator?

Though we may fall seven times, we will rise again. For it is the Lord who upholds us with His righteous right hand. Our Father, will never let us go. We are safe and secure in His loving arms.

The Lord our God is good. He will never forsake us. We are His children, and He will never abandon us. The enemy may say that we are forsaken, but we know the truth. For we know Who's we are, and we know in Whom we have trusted. Therefore, we know that we will never be left alone or forsaken, for we trust in our God, our Creator. Our God is merciful, and He freely gives. All of His children are blessed. I say, we are blessed just to know Him. To be called children of the Most High. For this alone, I am grateful.

Let us freely lend, without expecting to receive anything in return. For it is Jesus who said, "*And if you lend to those from whom you expect repayment, what credit is that to you? Even sinners lend to sinners, expecting to be repaid in full. But love your enemies, do good to them, and lend to them without expecting to get anything back. Then your reward will be great, and you will be children of the Most High, because he is kind to the ungrateful and wicked.*"

Depart from evil, and do good. The Lord loves justice, and He never forsakes those who belong to Him. No one can snatch us from Him, and nothing can separate us from His love. We are loved forevermore. We are wanted, forevermore. He does not forsake those who are His. We are preserved forever. We are sealed with the Holy Spirit of promise, and we await the day when we are called home, as we are but foreigners here on earth. This is not our home, only a temporary place of dwelling. The wicked will be cut off, but we will dwell with our God forever. How beautiful to dwell with our God, forever.

The mouth of the righteous speaks wisdom. We speak of what is right, and follow in the steps of our Lord Jesus Christ. The law of our God, is forever written in our hearts. We follow the path as His chosen, and even though it is hard and narrow, and even though sometimes we fall and we fail, we still follow. For our reward is not on this earth. We seek greater things, things that are unseen. So one may have to deal with the sorrow of this life, but we know that there is something, rather Someone, greater waiting for us. Therefore, we endure, knowing that we have an inheritance waiting for us, reserved for us in heaven, with the One who loves us dearly.

The wicked lie in wait. They watch the righteous, and seek to destroy them. They must be confused, for our God would never leave us in someone else's hands. Do they not know, that our God's grip is firm, and that no one can snatch us away from His hand? For one to think that they could take us from our God, must be confused.

I will wait on You Lord, and as I wait, I will continue to do what is right in Your eyes. I will not wander off and walk on my own path, instead, I will wait. Instead, I will walk in Your word. As I wait Lord, I vow to do good, and I will wait patiently, and I will wait expectantly. For You Lord, always come through for me. You will not forsake me, and You will never fail me. I ask this Lord, *Let the words of my mouth and the meditation of my heart Be acceptable in Your sight, O LORD, my strength and my Redeemer.*

May I please You with my life.

Even though the wicked may seem prosperous in their ways, they will soon pass away like chaff. They may seem to have power, riches, and fame, but their end will come, and they will be no more. You will seek them, and not find them. Therefore, do not idolize the wicked who have become famous, and do not wish you were like them, rich like them, and famous like them. Eventually, their day will come, and where will they be? The riches of this world are temporary. Therefore, place your treasures in a place where they do not fade away, and where no moth or rust can destroy them. The treasures of this life are but a breath, but the treasures of God, are eternal. For where your treasure is, there your heart will be also.

Instead of observing the wicked, observe the upright. Observe those who follow the Lord wholeheartedly. The future of that person is peace, and eternal life. But the sinners, those who follow this world, and those who reject Jesus Christ, they shall all be destroyed together. The future of the righteous is eternal life, and the future of the wicked is death. Who then, should you follow?

You Lord, are my strength and my song. My salvation Jesus, is through You, and You alone. In my times of trouble, You alone Lord, are my strength. You alone Lord, sustain me. You help me Lord, You deliver me. You deliver me from the wicked, from the plots of the evil. You alone

Lord, have the power to do this. You save me Lord, because I trust in You.

You would never give up on me, so therefore, I will never give up on You. I will remain steadfast, and I will remain firm. You Jesus, are my firm foundation, my anchor in this storm. In You, I will wait. In You, I will trust.

Psalm 40
Through my eyes

I wait patiently for You Lord. There are days when I feel my patience has worn thin, but You Lord, always lead me back to You. The Rock that is higher than I. You always hear me when I speak, Your face shines upon me. My Lord and my God. I will trust in Your promises, and I will trust in Your faithfulness. So many times You have brought me out of a horrible pit. So quick to say Lord, Lord, where are You? Yet, You remind me of Your faithfulness. How so many times, when my soul has been overwhelmed, and downcast within me, that You have calmed the storms inside me. Lord You listened, Lord You heard. You delivered me from turmoil, and from the pit that I was stuck in. You removed my feet from muddy clay, and placed them on the Rock, the Rock of my salvation. You don't just listen to Your children Lord, You act. You don't just hear, but You deliver. You establish my steps O Lord, and You put a new song in my mouth. A song of endless praise to my God. To my deliverer. Many will see Your deliverance O Lord, and be in awe of You. They will see the mighty hand of Our God, and trust Him.

Blessed are You, who put your full trust in the Lord. The one who does not honor the proud, as God opposes the proud, but shows favor to the humble. So shall we Lord, follow in Your footsteps, not giving our respect to the prideful.

Your works O Lord, are so wondrous and many. You have done so many good things Lord, so many wonderful things. I look at the trees Lord, and they sway back and forth, and I think Lord, who else could speak, and the wind obey them? Who else Lord, could make a seed, grow into a fruitful tree O God? Who could number my wonderings, hold the ocean in His hands, make a butterfly from a caterpillar, who Lord? Who can do all these things? Who could give daily food to the birds, and shelter to the squirrels? Who could take my sadness, and turn it to joy, and pain, and turn it to Your glory? There is none but You. Your works Lord, I see them all around me. They are so evident in my family, so clear in Your beauty. I could speak of all Your beauty Lord, but there are too many to count. Perhaps I would not have enough breath in me to recount them all. From the produce of the land, to the breath in my lungs O Lord. Everything is Yours. I Lord, am Yours. Your thoughts towards me Lord, are more than the grains of sand. How Lord, are You so mindful of us? We are but a breath. We are here today, and gone tomorrow. Yet You Lord, mighty and true, love us. Your thoughts are towards a people so much lower than You. You notice us in our insignificance, and You say, You are mine, I have called you. O Lord, my heart is forever Yours. My Lord and My God. How I love thee.

You did not ask for sacrifice, and You did not ask for payment. You did not desire or require these things from us. Instead, You gave. You gave Your love, and You gave Your life. You are mindful, to those who don't deserve

Your mindfulness. O Lord, You have opened my ears. My ears they hear, and my eyes they see. Lord, I will follow You all the days of my life, and thereafter. I delight in Your law Lord, and I live to please You. I am joyful to do Your will Lord, no matter the cost. Not as if I could ever repay You Lord, but because my love for You is true. I follow You not because of what I gain, but I follow because of who You are. My Savior and my God. I love You not for what I gain, for I count all as loss, and I pick up my cross, and I follow You Lord. I daily surrender Lord, and lay my hopes and dreams at Your feet. For You died for love, and I follow You for the same. I follow You because of the love I have for You in my heart.

I will proclaim Your name O Lord. The good news of Jesus Christ, I will proclaim. Whether it's a full assembly, or one person, I can not restrain my lips Lord. When they don't listen, I still have to speak. I can not restrain to tell others of Your love Lord. I can not hold back, even when their face is annoyed, I must speak of Your goodness, of Your love, and of Your faithfulness. How could one restrain such love that You give? How could one hold it back any longer? For who could restrain to speak of Your kindness Lord? When Your Spirit speaks to my heart Lord, how could I deny the truth that sets captives free? How can I not share of Your wondrous works? I can not. I can not restrain myself Lord.

Lord, do not withhold Your loving mercy from me. Your mercy, which I do not deserve, yet You freely give. Lord, let Your lovingkindness, and Your truth, continually preserve and guide me. Many troubles surround me Lord. My sins O Lord overtake me, so much so that I can not look up. I am filled with sorrow. I say that I will trust You, and then I fail, I say that I will not get angry when others come against me, but again, at times I fail. I am anxious, when I say that I won't be anxious, and I am sometimes worried for tomorrow, when You say to not. Lord, remember that I am but dust. When my heart fails me Lord, lead me to the Rock that is higher than I. When I am overwhelmed with sorrow Lord, be my comforter. Comfort me Lord, that I may comfort others with the same comfort in which You have so graciously given me. Be pleased Lord, to deliver Your servant. You know that my heart is for You Lord. Please, deliver me quickly.

Let those who seek to destroy me, be ashamed. Let them be brought to mutual confusion Lord. Let them be driven backward, and their plans not prosper against me. Those who wish evil upon me, let them be brought to dishonor. Let them be confused and dismayed, because of their shame.

Let all those who seek You Lord, rejoice and be glad in You. Let their heart rejoice at the sound of Your name, and let them sing joyful praises to You Lord. Let those who love You, who love Your salvation, say continually, the Lord be magnified. Let them lift Your name up Lord, for You are our hope and our strength, our firm foundation through all seasons. Even though I am poor and needy, the Lord looks upon me with love. He thinks about me, and loves me as I am. God, You are my help and my deliverer. There is none Lord, who can give me help like You. Do not delay Lord, please, deliver Your servant. My Lord and my God.

To see more books by Tentmaker Ministries, please go to Tm-ministries.com